Take a trip to ANTARCTICA

Keith Lye

Franklin Watts

Sydney

London New York Toronto

Facts about Antarctica

Area:
13,208,000 sq. km
(5,100,000 sq. miles)

Volume of ice:
Antarctica is buried
under about 29 million
cubic km (7 million cubic
miles) of ice. The
greatest thickness of ice
is 4.78 km (2.97 miles)
in Wilkes Land

Highest peak:
Vinson Massif, 5,139 m
(16,860 ft)

Lowest temperature:
− 89.2°C (− 128.6°F).
This temperature, the
world's lowest screen
temperature, was
recorded at a Russian
scientific station on July
21, 1983

Exploration:
The first certain landing
in Antarctica did not
take place until 1831.
The first man to reach
the South Pole was
Roald Amundsen, a
Norwegian, on
December 14, 1911

Franklin Watts Limited
12a Golden Square
London W1

ISBN: UK Edition 0 86313 092 5
ISBN: US Edition 0 531 04514 5
Library of Congress Catalog
Card No: 83–50997
© Franklin Watts Limited 1984
Reprinted 1984

Typeset by Ace Filmsetting Ltd,
Frome, Somerset
Printed in Hong Kong

Text Editor: Brenda Williams
Maps: Tony Payne
Design: Mushroom Production
Photographs: British Antarctic Survey;
Zefa, 3–6, 17, 22, 27, 28, 30; Graham
Wilson, 7, 10, 12; Charles Swithinbank,
10; Novosti Press Agency, 13; Mansell
Collection, 21
Front and Back Covers: Graham Wilson

Antarctica is the world's fifth largest
continent. It is bigger than those of
Europe or Oceania. But Antarctica
is so cold that nobody lives there,
apart from a few scientists who work
there for short periods. Nearly all of
Antarctica is buried by snow and ice.

Parts of Antarctica are claimed by Argentina, Australia, Britain, Chile, France, New Zealand and Norway. But there is no general agreement on their claims. King George Island is in the South Shetland Islands, in the British Antarctic Territory.

An ice-breaker cuts a channel through pack-ice in the Ross Sea off the Ross Ice Shelf. Ice shelves are large sheets of floating ice which are joined to the ice on the shore. These shelves border many Antarctic coasts.

High cliffs of ice line the coasts
in many places. Large chunks of ice
break away from the land to form
icebergs. These icebergs float north,
away from Antarctica.

Many icebergs from Antarctica
have flat tops and steep-sided cliffs.
The world's biggest known iceberg
came from Antarctica. It covered an
area larger than Belgium.

Mount Erebus is the only active volcano in Antarctica. It was discovered in 1841 by a Scottish explorer, Sir James Clark Ross, and named after one of his ships.

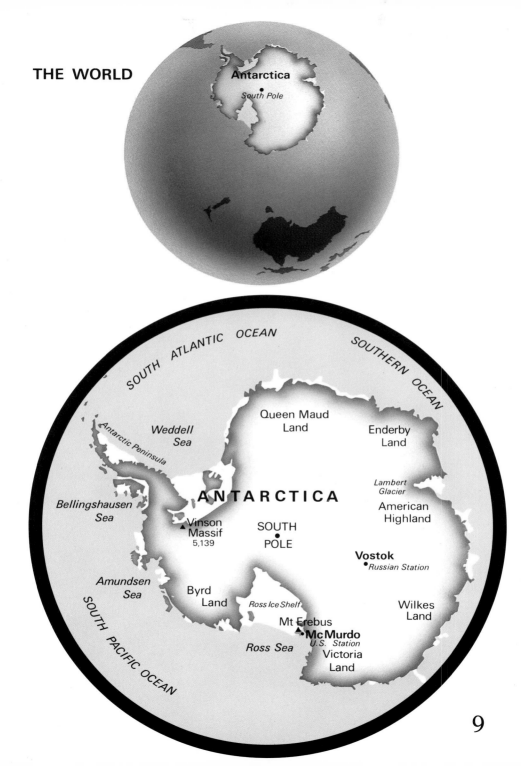

THE WORLD

Antarctica
• South Pole

SOUTH ATLANTIC OCEAN

SOUTHERN OCEAN

Queen Maud
Land

Weddell
Sea

Antarctic Peninsula

Enderby
Land

ANTARCTICA

Lambert
Glacier

American
Highland

Bellingshausen
Sea

▲ Vinson
Massif
5,139

SOUTH
•
POLE

Vostok
• Russian Station

Amundsen
Sea

Byrd
Land

Ross Ice Shelf

Wilkes
Land

SOUTH PACIFIC OCEAN

Mt Erebus
▲ • McMurdo
U.S. Station

Ross Sea

Victoria
Land

9

Antarctica is the coldest continent
on Earth. At times there are fierce
storms, called blizzards. When these
storm winds blow, they whip up loose
snow into the air.

10

Besides the seven countries which claim parts of Antarctica, others have research stations there. Russia and the USA are among them. These scientists are wearing wind-proof clothes, warm boots, and mitts.

McMurdo Station is Antarctica's largest research base. It is run by the USA. A nuclear reactor has been built there. There is also a desalination plant which makes fresh water from seawater.

Vostok Station is one of Russia's inland science research stations. Scientists of many nations are based in Antarctica. They work together in a friendly way.

Travel in Antarctica is difficult. In the ice there are gaps called crevasses which are dangerous when hidden by snow. Here a sno-cat, a special kind of tractor, crosses a crevasse.

Scientists who study weather are called meteorologists. At the research stations they check weather conditions regularly. Because the Earth is tilted, there is daylight all the time at the South Pole for half of the year and darkness for the other six months.

Geologists study rocks in the mountains which jut through the ice in the Antarctic Peninsula. Research by geologists may one day lead to mining works in Antarctica.

16

Scientists who work at research stations in Antarctica rely on the outside world for all their supplies, including those for food and heating.

Some scientists work below ground. This is the entrance to an underground British observatory. Here, scientists record such things as earthquakes.

Many scientists live in heated houses, but some have homes under the ice. This research station is in the South Orkney Islands, in the British Antarctic Territory. It is used by biologists.

A mechanic repairs a motor toboggan, or snowmobile. Care must be taken with all equipment. It may be months before spare parts arrive.

The Norwegian explorer Roald Amundsen led the first expedition to reach the South Pole. He arrived there on December 14, 1911, and returned safely. A British expedition led by Captain Robert Falcon Scott reached the Pole on January 18, 1912. But all the men died on the way back.

Amundsen's expedition used husky dogs, like those seen here, to draw their sledges. Scott used ponies, which all died. Scott and his men then had to pull their own sledges. This slowed their expedition down.

The Trans-Antarctic Expedition of 1957–8 made the first land crossing of the continent. The expedition was led by Vivian Fuchs, a British scientist (right). With him at the Pole are Edmund Hillary, the climber of Everest (middle) and George Dufek, an American admiral (left).

The Trans-Antarctic Expedition of
1957–8 did much scientific research.
The depth of ice was measured by
studying seismic (earthquake) waves
set off by explosions in the ice.

Most of Antarctica has no plants or animals. But the seas around the continent are rich in life, including the rare southern right whales. These whales were hunted until they almost died out. Hunting is now banned and their numbers are growing again.

Penguins live around the coasts of
Antarctica. The largest is the
Emperor penguin. This colony lives
on the southeast coast of the Weddell
Sea. Penguins cannot fly, but these
birds are superb swimmers.

Adélie penguins are the most common of the five kinds of penguins which live in Antarctica. Many flying birds, including fulmars, petrels and skuas, also live in Antarctica.

The Arctic tern breeds in the Arctic lands of the north. As summer ends, it flies south to Antarctica. So this amazing bird enjoys two summers a year. In their flight around the world, some terns cover 35,400 km (22,000 miles) in nine months.

Six kinds of seals live around
Antarctica. They are crab-eater seals,
elephant seals, fur seals, leopard
seals, Ross seals and Weddell seals.
This is a Weddell seal pup.

The shortest route from the sea to the South Pole is across the Ross Ice Shelf. But travel on foot over the snow and ice can be difficult.

Stormy seas, pack-ice and bitterly cold weather are all dangers on sea journeys to Antarctica. This bleak continent is still a remote place. But research there has told us much about the Earth's history, the world's climate and life in the southern seas.

Index